pharaoh
KING OF EGYPT

pharaoh
KING OF EGYPT

MARGARET MAITLAND

THE BRITISH MUSEUM PRESS

Wig from a royal statue
Thebes, Egypt. 1550–1186 BC.
Faience and gold, H 10 cm, W 9.5 cm

Originally part of a statue, this wig with
gold ornamental crown expresses the
alleged divinity of the king. The blue
faience imitates the precious stone lapis
lazuli, which was said to form the hair of
the gods.

This book is published to accompany the touring exhibition
Pharaoh: King of Egypt at Birmingham Museum and Art Gallery
from 7 July to 14 October 2012; Kelvingrove Art Gallery and
Museum, Glasgow from 3 November to 24 February 2013; and
Bristol Museum and Art Gallery from 15 March to 9 June 2013.

Margaret Maitland has asserted the right to be identified
as the author of this work.

First published in 2012 by The British Museum Press
A division of The British Museum Company Ltd
38 Russell Square, London WC1B 3QQ
britishmuseum.org/publishing

A catalogue record for this book is available from
the British Library.

ISBN   978-0-7141-1998-4

Designed by Price Watkins
Printed in Malaysia

Frontispiece: Relief fragment depicting sun-disc and crown
(detail). Temple of Mentuhotep II, Deir el-Bahri, Thebes, Egypt,
2055–2004 BC. Limestone, H 36.5, W 26.5 cm

The majority of objects illustrated in this book are from the
collection of the British Museum. Their Museum inventory
numbers are listed on page 95. Futher information about the
Museum and its collection can be found at britishmuseum.org

Contents

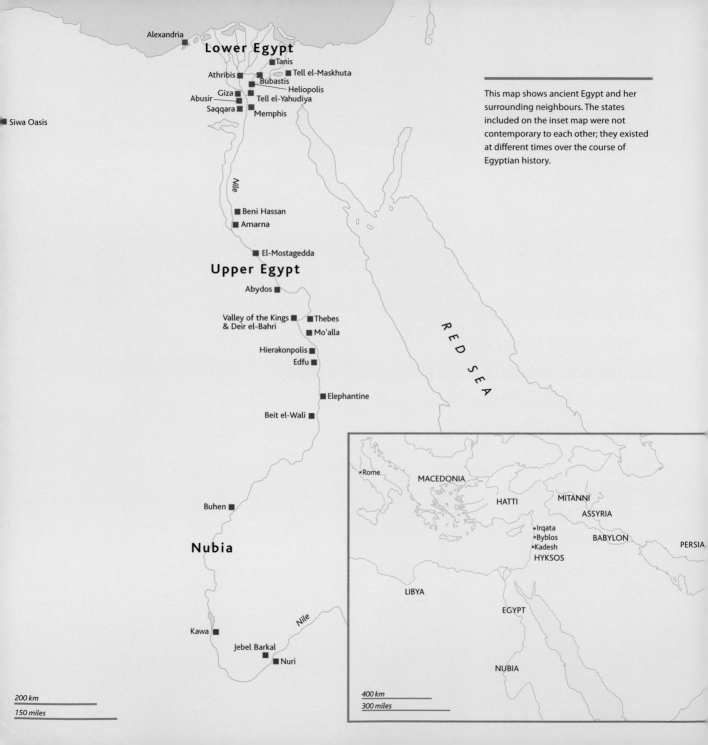

Alexandria

Lower Egypt

Tanis

Tell el-Maskhuta

Athribis

Bubastis

Heliopolis

Giza

Abusir

Tell el-Yahudiya

Saqqara

Memphis

Siwa Oasis

Nile

Beni Hassan

Amarna

El-Mostagedda

Upper Egypt

Abydos

Valley of the Kings
& Deir el-Bahri

Thebes

Mo'alla

Hierakonpolis

Edfu

Elephantine

Beit el-Wali

R E D   S E A

Buhen

Nubia

Kawa

Jebel Barkal

Nuri

This map shows ancient Egypt and her surrounding neighbours. The states included on the inset map were not contemporary to each other; they existed at different times over the course of Egyptian history.

Rome

MACEDONIA

HATTI

MITANNI

ASSYRIA

Irqata

Byblos

Kadesh

BABYLON

PERSIA

HYKSOS

LIBYA

EGYPT

NUBIA

200 km

150 miles

400 km

300 miles

Introduction

'The sun god Ra placed (the) King in the land of the living for eternity and all time; for judging men, for making gods content, for creating ma'at *(truth), for destroying evil'*

King as Sunpriest

Over the course of more than three thousand years of ancient Egyptian civilization the mantle of kingship changed hands countless times, but the primary duties of the pharaohs remained constant: to act as pious priests, devoted to serving the gods, and as mighty warriors, extending Egypt's borders as well as safeguarding order within them.

The responsibilities of the pharaohs were supposedly to serve the people of Egypt, but inevitably they became interested in maintaining power for themselves, and this was incorporated into their role. By acting as chief priest to the gods, the pharaoh could present his rule as divinely sanctioned, and in defending Egypt the king could obtain valuable foreign resources and enhance his own political power. In reality, the defence of Egypt's borders was not always as successful as her kings hoped or portrayed; foreigners held the throne for roughly a third of ancient Egyptian history – over a thousand years in total.

This book examines the ideals of Egyptian kingship, the mythology of divine rule and the image pharaohs sought to present to their subjects, and contrasts these with the actual

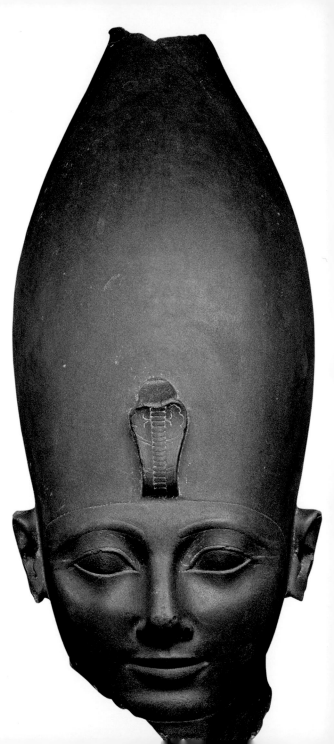

Head of Thutmose III
Karnak, Thebes, Egypt. 1479–57 BC.
Green siltstone, H 60.5 cm, W 19 cm

individuals who wore the crown and the realities of their reigns. Each chapter addresses a different aspect of the pharaoh's idealized image and the responsibilities of the king: as 'the son of Ra', supposedly descended from the gods, but often crowned through circumstance, conspiracy or invasion; as 'the Lord of the Two Lands', responsible for maintaining order and the unity of Upper and Lower Egypt, though their failure sometimes plunged the country into civil war; as high priest to the gods, building temples for their worship, or rather taking the shortcut of reusing older monuments; as warrior-king, supposedly protecting Egypt from her enemies, but being conquered in turn just as often; and as 'Lord of Eternity', when the pharaoh was buried and thought to become one with the gods, after which he might subsequently be worshipped, maligned or forgotten.

Above all, the chief duty of the king was to uphold *ma'at* – an Egyptian concept encapsulating order, balance and justice. *Ma'at* was bestowed on the universe by the gods, but it needed to be maintained, chiefly by the king, by preserving stability, protecting the country from foreign threats and pleasing the gods. The concept of

Defaced royal coffin
Tomb 55, Valley of the
Kings, Thebes, Egypt.
1336 BC. Wood, gold and
semi-precious stones,
H 135 cm, L 370 cm
Egyptian Museum, Cairo

Book of the Dead papyrus with version of the text known as 'King as Sunpriest' Egypt. 1295–1069 BC.
Papyrus, H 31.1 cm, W 30.6 cm

King list (part of)
Temple of Ramses II, Abydos, Egypt. *c.* 1250 BC.
Painted limestone, H 135 cm, L 370 cm

ma'at was also useful to the pharaoh in maintaining control over his subjects: ordinary people were expected to uphold *ma'at* in their everyday lives by conforming to society and being loyal, law-abiding citizens.

The pharaohs mobilized extensive resources to perfect an iconic, idealized image of themselves as flawless and all-powerful in order to convince entire populations that they were chosen for greatness by the gods. The green siltstone head of Thutmose III wearing the crown of Upper Egypt (p. 8) demonstrates the physical perfection achieved in depictions of the king through the masterful technique of royal craftsmen.

However, neither the pharaoh nor his

reputation was invincible, as the fate of a royal coffin from the Valley of the Kings indicates (p. 9). Possibly belonging to one of Egypt's most controversial pharaohs, Akhenaten, or his short-lived successor Smenkhkara, the coffin has been defaced: its golden mask violently ripped off and the owner's name hacked out. Akhenaten was so despised for his heresy of abandoning Egypt's traditional gods in favour of a new religion that officials under the pharaoh Tutankhamun, his son, sought to wipe his memory from history.

Numerous pharaohs did not fit the Egyptian ideal – many women, usurpers and foreigners sat on the throne, most of whom the Egyptians sought to forcefully remove from history. Some of our best sources of information on the pharaohs come from king lists (p. 11), which record the sequence of rulers and the length of their reigns. These were not compiled as objective historical records, but rather to present the ruling monarch as the rightful heir to a long line of royal ancestors. As such, king lists selectively excluded any pharaohs who did not conform to the ideal, including female rulers, such as Sobekneferu and Hatshepsut, the foreign Hyksos kings who invaded from the Near East and contested kings who ruled during times of civil war.

Although powerful female pharaohs might not fit the ideal image of ruler, many kings relied on the women closest to them for support in ruling Egypt. Some even left their wives or mothers in charge of the entire country when they were away on military campaigns. Queen Tiy carried out diplomatic correspondence with foreign kings, and Queen Ahhotep, mother of King Ahmose, was praised by her son as 'one who cares for Egypt. She has looked after her (Egypt's) soldiers; she has guarded her'.

Pharaohs were always depicted standing as equals before the gods: god-like in their physical perfection, strength and beauty. Yet in reality they were still very human: for example, a letter written by the boy King Pepi II conveys his childish excitement at the prospect of seeing dancing pygmies, and analysis of the mummy of elderly Ramses II reveals that he dyed his hair in his old age.

Even the deification of the pharaoh after death could combine the sublime and the ridiculous. Deceased kings were worshipped, and some were even treated like saints. But as people prayed to them to intercede on their behalf from beyond the grave, the king was reduced to passing judgement in banal price disputes and cases of stolen cows and missing shirts, for example: 'The chisel-bearer Ka-ha called to King Amenhotep, saying "My good lord, come today, because my two garments have been stolen!"'.

Looking beyond the pharaohs' dazzling golden image to the broader archaeological evidence and reading between the lines, we can examine the realities of their fascinating, sometimes controversial, lives and their impact on Egypt and the wider ancient world.

Chronology of pharaohs

This chronology presents the main time periods of Egyptian history as divided by Egyptologists. The list of pharaohs is not complete, but rather a selection of those who are mentioned in the text along with their approximate regnal dates.

Early Dynastic Period (c. 3100–2686 BC)

Ist Dynasty
c. 3100 BC Narmer
c. 3000 BC Djer
c. 2950 BC Den

Old Kingdom (c. 2686–2181 BC)

4th Dynasty
2589–2566 BC Khufu

6th Dynasty
2278–2184 BC Pepi II

First Intermediate Period (c. 2160–2050 BC)

Middle Kingdom (c. 2050–1650 BC)

11th Dynasty
2055–2004 BC Mentuhotep II
1992–1985 BC Mentuhotep VI

12th Dynasty
1985–1955 BC Amenemhat I
1965–1920 BC Senusret I
1880–1874 BC Senusret II
1874–1855 BC Senusret III
1808–1799 BC Amenemhat IV
1799–1795 BC Queen Sobekneferu

Second Intermediate Period (c. 1650–1550 BC)

17th Dynasty
c. 1570 BC Sobekemzaf II
c. 1560 BC Seqenenra Taa II and
            Queen Ahhotep

New Kingdom (c. 1550–1069 BC)

18th Dynasty
1550–1525 BC Ahmose
1525–1504 BC Amenhotep I and
              Queen Ahmose-Nefertari
1504–1492 BC Thutmose I
1492–1479 BC Thutmose II
1479–1457 BC Hatshepsut
1479–1425 BC Thutmose III
1390–1352 BC Amenhotep III and
              Queen Tiy
1352–1336 BC Akhenaten
1337–1336? BC Smenkhkara
1336–1327 BC Tutankhamun and
              Queen Ankhesenamun
1327–1323 BC Ay
1323–1295 BC Horemheb

19th Dynasty
1295–1294 BC Ramses I
1294–1279 BC Seti I
1279–1213 BC Ramses II

20th Dynasty
1184–1153 BC Ramses III
1126–1108 BC Ramses IX

Third Intermediate Period (c. 1069–747 BC)

21st Dynasty
1054–1036 BC Pinudjem I

Late Period (c. 747–332 BC)

25th Dynasty
716–702 BC Shakabo
690–664 BC Taharqa

27th Dynasty
522–486 BC Darius I

30th Dynasty
360–343 BC Nectanebo II

Ptolemaic Period (c. 332–30 BC)

Macedonian Kings
332–323 BC Alexander the Great

Ptolemaic Period
205–180 BC Ptolemy V Epiphanes and
            Queen Cleopatra I
180–145 BC Ptolemy VI Philometor
80–51 BC Ptolemy XII Neos Dionysos
51–30 BC Cleopatra II Philopator

Roman Period (30 BC–AD 306)

AD 14–37 Tiberius

River Nile, Beni Hassan

View of the River Nile today, centre of the ancient Egyptian world, with the distinction between the fertile agricultural fields and barren desert clearly visible. In the south, the Nile runs along a strip of land between high desert cliffs, while in the north it divides into many branches spread over a wide plain.

*'I am come as Horus. The land was given to me;
I am its lord, one who contents god with what
he gave. I am his son, his protector'*

Building inscription of King Senusret I

Son of the sun god

*'In our opinion, Alexander the king of the
Macedonians was the best and most noble of
men…many say that he was the son of King
Philip, but they are deceivers. This is untrue: he
was not Philip's son, but the wisest of the
Egyptians say that he was the son of
Nectanebo'*

Greek Alexander Romance

Son of the sun god

'Horus', 'son of the sun god Ra', 'beloved of the goddess Ma'at', 'divine of birth', 'chosen of the god Amun': each king of Egypt was hailed by numerous titles, names and epithets signalling his divine birth, predestined right to rule and support and protection from the gods.

Each king was thought to follow in the footsteps of the gods who had served as the first rulers of Egypt. In mythology, the god Osiris ruled as first pharaoh, but his brother Seth murdered him for the throne. Osiris' devoted wife Isis raised their son Horus in hiding until he was old enough to avenge his father's death and claim the throne from Seth. Subsequent kings were all identified with the god Horus, for whom they acted as an earthly representative. However, the pharaoh was not fully considered a god himself until after his death when he was united with the god Osiris, and his son (or heir) went on to become the next incarnation of Horus. In reality royal succession was not always as smooth as this.

Ideally, the pharaoh was the first-born son of the previous king, thus both Egyptian and male. But the high mortality rates of ancient times robbed many kings of their sons, leaving the role to be filled by the closest remaining relative, such as a brother or nephew, or sometimes a female relative or even a government official.

The young king Tutankhamun died before reaching the age of twenty with no heirs to succeed him – his two stillborn children were buried with him in his tomb. His desperate widow Ankhesenamun took the extreme step of writing to a foreign ruler, the Hittite king: 'My husband died. I do not have a son. But, they say, many are your sons. If you would give me one of your sons, he would become my husband'. But the Hittite prince was murdered on route to Egypt and Tutankhamun's vizier Ay took the throne instead.

Inlaid pendant depicting a winged scarab beetle holding a sun-disc Egypt. 1880–1874 BC. Electrum, lapis lazuli, carnelian and feldspar, L 3.5 cm, W 1.8 cm

This pendant's decorative elements double as hieroglyphs spelling out the name of King Senusret II. When a king took the throne, he adopted four new names in addition to his birth name. These names were entire phrases that indicated a king's relationship with certain gods, emphasized his power by praising his strength or associating him with legendary kings of the past and set out an agenda for his reign, such as war or new beginnings.

The frequent claims in Egyptian texts that the pharaoh was destined to rule 'from the egg' and 'conquered in the womb' were clearly not true. Unusual successions could be engineered by conspiracies within the royal family, assassinations or foreign invasions. The divine royal birth was especially emphasized by kings from more doubtful origins who wanted to assert their right to the throne. Pharaoh Hatshepsut, though not the first woman to rule over Egypt, was the first female to lay claim to the fully-fledged role of king. Masculine traits were adopted in depictions of Hatshepsut and perhaps significantly she offered pictorial evidence of her divine birth. On a wall of her temple at Deir el-Bahri the sun god is shown disguising himself as her father King Thutmose I in order to impregnate her mother, and the birth is assisted by a group of deities. Hatshepsut's rule could never tally with the ideals of Egyptian kingship though, and shortly after her reign her name and image were systematically erased from her monuments.

Despite not being seen by their people as living deities, pharaohs were considered to be under the special protection of the gods. In representations of battle, the king is accompanied by the falcon form of the god Horus, or the vulture goddess of Upper Egypt, Nekhbet, hovering protectively over the pharaoh. But this divine protection did not make the king invulnerable; the son of Ra was not immortal. The poem 'The Teaching of King Amenemhat', tells of the assassination of the pharaoh, who speaks to his son from beyond the grave in a dream. As Amenemhat I admits in the poem, 'no one is strong in the night; no one can fight alone'. The concept of kingship might be divinely eternal but the pharaoh himself was, in the end, mortal.

Figurine of the goddess Isis nursing her son Horus

Egypt. 664–332 BC. Bronze, H 23.6 cm, W 5.4 cm

Isis was the classic Egyptian mother goddess. Her relationship with her son Horus, identified with the living king, was used to justify the divine succession of the pharaohs. Isis was an important protectress of the king, but ordinary Egyptians also sought her and Horus' help for their healing powers and this statue may have been donated to a temple for that purpose.

Statue of the god Ra-Horakhty
Tell el-Maskhuta, Egypt. 1279–1213 BC.
Granite, H 94 cm, W 39 cm

Royal names were written in oval shapes
known as cartouches, symbolizing eternity.
Here, the cartouche of Ramses II is protected
by Ra-Horakhty, a deity incorporating both
Ra, the sun god, and Horus, the falcon god
of kingship.

Relief fragment depicting sun-disc and crown

Temple of Mentuhotep II, Deir el-Bahri, Thebes, Egypt. 2055–2004 BC.
Painted limestone,
H 36.5 cm, W 26.5 cm

The sun god gave the pharaoh life, power and protection. Above the pharaoh's crown is a winged sun-disc with *uraei* and *ankh*-signs.

haraohs were known as the 'son of Ra', emphasizing the divine descent that justified their rule. This title usually passed from father to son, but not all kings inherited the throne. Horemheb was an army general before he became pharaoh. After his coronation he built a royal tomb in the Valley of the Kings, but still amended the images of himself as a commoner in his original tomb by adding the *uraeus* to his brow (as seen here, right).

Relief fragment with the inscription 'son of Ra'
(above) Tomb of Pharaoh Seti I, Valley of the Kings, Thebes, Egypt. 1294–1279 BC. Limestone, L 29 cm, H 22 cm

Doorjamb from the tomb of General Horemheb
(right) Saqqara, Egypt. 1323–1295 BC. Limestone, H 182 cm, W 42 cm

Pharaohs associated themselves with Amun-Ra, king of the gods, to stress their legitimacy, but invading foreign rulers simply followed this example. When Alexander the Great conquered Egypt in 332 BC, he sought out the Oracle of Amun at Siwa Oasis where the god allegedly acknowledged the Macedonian-Greek ruler as his son. Alexander and his successors were depicted in both Egyptian and Greek (Hellenistic) style.

Figurine of the god Amun-Ra
Karnak, Thebes, Egypt. 1069–727 BC.
Gold and silver, H 24 cm, W 5 cm

**Head in the style of
Alexander the Great
from a statuette**
Temple of Aphrodite, Cyrene, Libya.
300–100 BC. Marble, H 10 cm

Figurine of a royal woman

Egypt. 760–656 BC. Bronze with gold and silver inlays, H 21.5 cm

Royal women could wield considerable authority. This figurine probably represents a 'God's Wife of Amun', a high priestess role performed by the king's daughter, which held substantial political importance during the eighth to seventh centuries BC.

Stela with cartouches of Pharaohs Thutmose III and Hatshepsut

Wadi Halfa, Sudan. 1479–1425 BC. Sandstone, H 65 cm, W 42 cm

Kings were supposedly the 'son of Ra', so a female pharaoh did not fit the royal ideal. When her husband, Pharaoh Thutmose II, died Hatshepsut at first shared power with her stepson Thutmose III, who was too young to rule, but she then proceeded to crown herself pharaoh. After her death, monuments bearing her name and titles were defaced or destroyed. On this stela her cartouche has been erased while that of Thutmose III is left intact.

Statue of Senenmut
Karnak, Thebes, Egypt. 1479–1472 BC.
Granodiorite, H 72.5 cm, W 24 cm

The high official Senenmut holds Princess
Neferura, the only daughter of Pharaohs
Thutmose II and Hatshepsut. She may have
been designated as her mother's successor
before Thutmose III took back the throne.

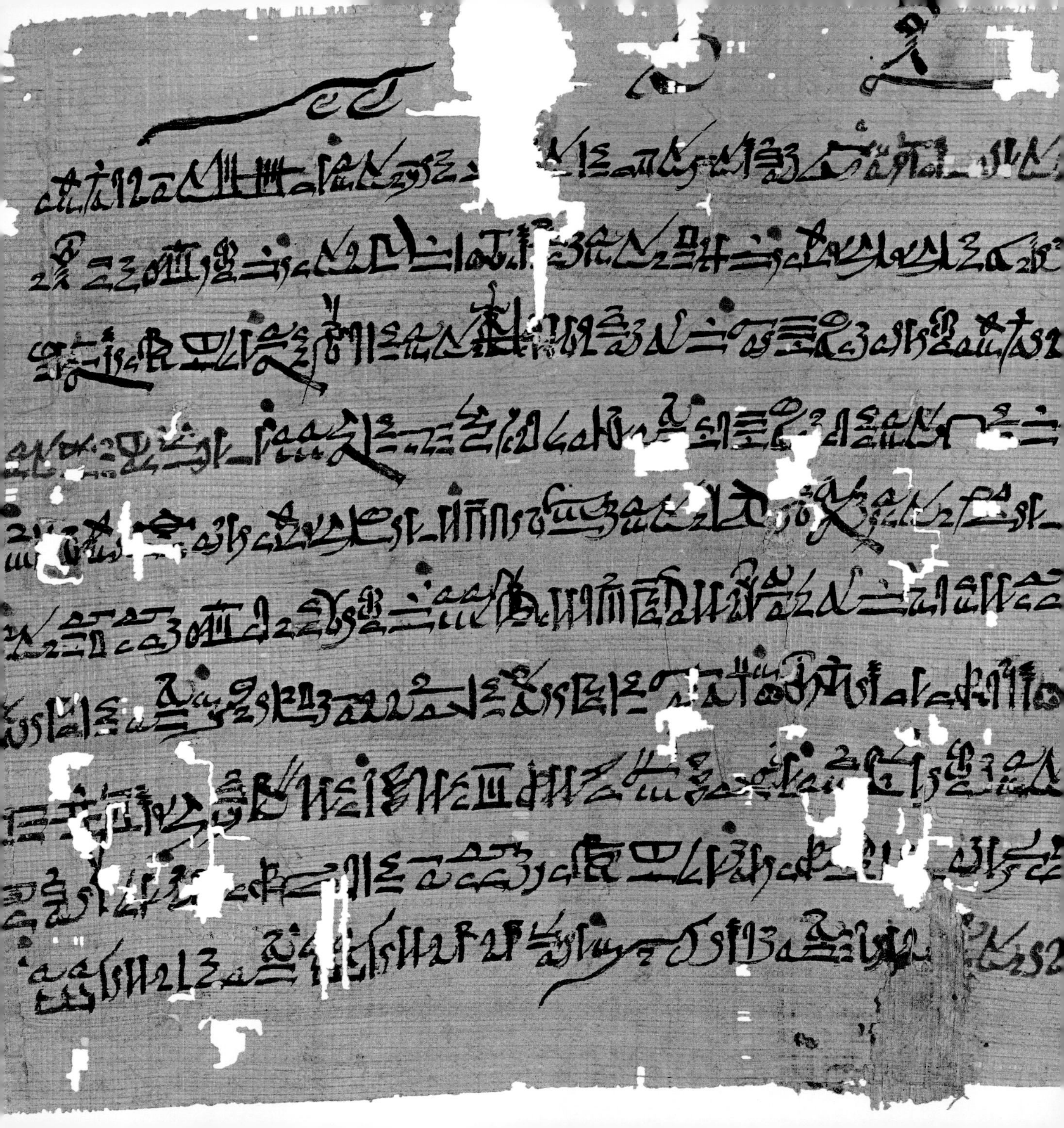

Papyrus with the poem 'The Teaching of Amenemhat'

Egypt. 1295–1186 BC. Papyrus,
L 29.5 cm, H 21.5 cm

'Divinely appointed', pharaohs were generally depicted as faultless and unassailable, but literature provided a way in which their subjects could question or even criticize their role. In this poem, the deceased Pharaoh Amenemhat I speaks to his son in a dream, telling of his own assassination and giving advice on how to be a better king.

Relief of Ptolemaic Queen and son

Egypt. 180–145 BC. Limestone,
L 19 cm, W 15.6 cm

During the Macedonian-Greek Ptolemaic dynasty, royal women were politically important and participated in brother-sister marriage. This relief may represent Queen Cleopatra I and her son Ptolemy VI, who ruled Egypt alongside his mother before marrying his sister Cleopatra II.

Standard forms for depicting the pharaoh were established early in Egyptian history and changed very little over time, emphasizing the timeless nature of the role. Although both statues exhibit the same striding pose, striped cloth *nemes* headdress with *uraeus*, and royal *shendyt*-kilt, the statue pictured on the right in fact depicts a Greek pharaoh of Egypt who ruled over 1300 years after Mentuhotep VI, shown on the left.

Unfinished statue of a Ptolemaic pharaoh (above right)
Athribis, Egypt. 305–30 BC. Basalt, H 105 cm, W 28 cm

Statue of Pharaoh Mentuhotep VI (left)
Karnak, Thebes, Egypt. 1675–1550 BC.
Green schist, H 22.5 cm

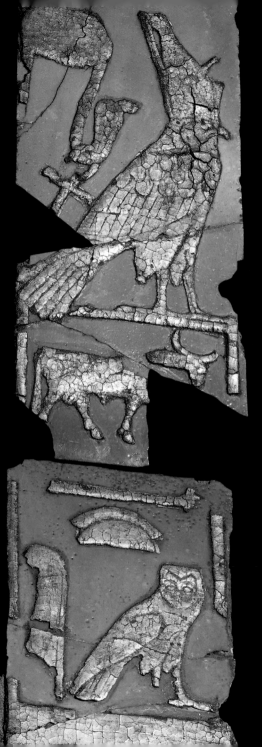

Tiles with the titles of Pharaoh Amenhotep III

Egypt. 1390–1352 BC. Faience and gold, L 18–23 cm

When a pharaoh took the throne he adopted four new
names in addition to his original birth name to emphasize
his divine right to rule. These tiles list the names of
Amenhotep III, which means 'The god Amun is satisfied'.

*'A king from the south will come, called Ameny.
He will take the White Crown; he will uplift the
Red Crown. He will unite the Two Powers…
Truth will return to its proper place, with Chaos
driven outside'*

The Words of Neferti

Lord of the Two Lands

---

*'Laughter is ruined, and [no longer] sounds.
There is only groaning throughout the land…
Look, the land has begun to be despoiled of
kingship, by a few people who know no
counsels, look they have fallen to rebellion, and
the royal residence has collapsed in a single
moment'*

The Dialogue of Ipuwer and the Lord of All

Lord of the Two Lands

When the kingdom of Egypt emerged around 3100 BC, forged from two distinct areas along the River Nile, its origins quickly became steeped in a mythology that was used to justify the rule of a single king over the entire country. Geographically, the Egyptian landscape can be divided into two regions: in the south, the Nile valley, a thin narrow strip of fertile land on either side of the river, often flanked by high desert cliffs, and to the north, the Delta region, where the Nile branches out into a network of channels across a wide fertile plain. It was once thought that these two areas represented distinct kingdoms during Egypt's earliest history, unified when the southern ruler conquered the north. However, the archaeological record suggests that the process may not have been so simple, and that the culture from the south slowly spread across Egypt over several hundred years.

Regardless of what actually happened, the Egyptians themselves thought of their country as a nation made up of two lands bound together only through the strength of the king, without whom the country would descend into chaos. The pharaoh was called 'the Lord of the Two Lands', and was depicted wearing the dual crown, which combined the crowns associated with Upper and Lower Egypt. When celebrating their jubilee, kings were required to prove their ability to keep the Two Lands united by performing a ritual run around boundary markers representing the borders of Egypt.

In a land defined by the reliability of the annual Nile flood, a place that guarded traditions for millennia, the Egyptians valued order above all. Upholding *ma'at* was the most important role the pharaoh played and keeping Egypt united was considered key to maintaining order. The king was portrayed as the sole person with the ability to do this, but in reality numerous people helped him in government.

Tile with the royal title 'Lord of the Two Lands'
Tell el-Yahudiya, Egypt. 1184–1153 BC. Faience, L 13 cm, W 8.4 cm
This tile originally decorated a palace of Ramses III.

The administration of such a vast territory could only be undertaken with the aid of a massive state bureaucracy, including national, provincial and local levels of government. To ensure the loyalty of his most powerful officials the king rewarded them with titles, land, gold, statues and imported goods. For the most part these officials served as the foundation of the pharaoh's power, but at times when the office of the king was weakened, their strength grew and the unity of the Two Lands fell. Control of the country was at times divided amongst competing ambitious local leaders, each calling themselves 'king', leaving the country vulnerable to foreign invasion.

A local governor, Ankhtifi of Mo'alla,

portrayed his role in Egypt's first civil war (c. 2160–2050 BC), in which he conquered two neighbouring provinces, as that of a king reunifying the country: 'Horus brought me to Edfu to re-establish it…I found it inundated like marshland, abandoned by him who belonged to it, in the grip of a rebel, under the control of a wretch'. Although Egyptian literature paints the period as a chaotic dark age, the decentralization of power and redistribution of wealth may not have been entirely bad for the general population and may have resulted in an increase in social mobility and literacy.

Egypt's first civil war shook the traditional concept of kingship, but when the local Theban ruler Mentuhotep II finally succeeded in reunifying the country, it simply reinforced and strengthened the mythology. Subsequent kings sought to associate themselves with Mentuhotep II by glorifying his achievement of reuniting the Two Lands.

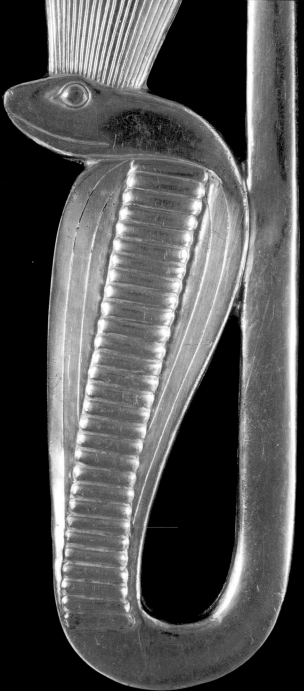

Furniture ornament in the form of a cobra

Egypt. 664–332 BC. Gold, L 13.6 cm

The cobra goddess, Wadjet, represented Lower Egypt and is depicted here wearing the red crown symbolic of that region. Her counterpart in Upper Egypt was the vulture goddess Nekhbet. These goddesses were thought to protect the king as he sought to maintain order and balance in the Two Lands.

Figurine of Ma'at

Egypt. 664–332 BC. Bronze, H 27 cm, W 4.6 cm

This figurine depicts the goddess Ma'at, the personification of order, balance and justice. Along with offerings of food and drink the king presented figurines of Ma'at to gods in the temples.

Replica of the Narmer Palette
Hierakonpolis, Egypt. 3100–2890 BC.
Original of greywacke stone, H 64 cm, W 42 cm

One of the earliest kings of Egypt, Narmer
was renowned for having brought about the
unification of Upper and Lower Egypt, though
there may not have been one decisive battle.
Narmer is shown on one side of this palette
inspecting decapitated adversaries while
wearing the red crown (left), while the other
side shows him in the white crown killing
enemies (right).

Hatshepsut performing the *sed*-festival run
Red Chapel, Karnak Temple, Thebes, Egypt. 1479–1457 BC. Red granite

The jubilee *sed*-festival celebrated thirty years of a pharaoh's rule and included a ceremony in which the monarch had to prove their continuing ability to unite and defend Egypt. Here female Pharaoh Hatshepsut is shown as a man running around boundary markers, which represent the borders of Egypt, accompanied by a bull symbolizing royal strength.

Label depicting scenes of a *sed*-festival for King Den
Abydos, Egypt. 3050–2890 BC. Ebony, L 8 cm, W 5.5 cm

The image in the top right-hand corner of this label is one of the earliest representations of the *sed*-festival run (top right) and the first depiction of the dual crown of Upper and Lower Egypt. Some kings celebrated their jubilee early or multiple times to strengthen their claim to the throne.

Block statue of Sennefer

Thebes, Egypt. 1479–1425 BC. Granodiorite, H 90 cm, W 38 cm

Sennefer held the important position of Overseer of Seal Bearers under Pharaoh Thutmose III. Kings attempted to ensure the loyalty of their key officials by offering them elaborate titles, estates and rich rewards, such as the costly stone used to make this statue.

Ostracon depicting Ramses IX with prince and vizier

Valley of the Kings, Thebes, Egypt. 1126 –1108 BC.
Limestone, H 48.3 cm, L 76.3 cm

The pharaoh was presented as Egypt's sole unifying force, but the king actually relied on a huge state bureaucracy to manage the governance of the country. This ostracon shows Ramses IX (left) with the crown prince and the vizier.

Shabti of Pinudjem I

Egypt. 978–959 BC. Faience, H 13.7 cm

Powerful officials could threaten the authority of the king. Pinudjem I, a general and high priest of Amun, controlled southern Egypt from Thebes, while the pharaoh based at Tanis ruled the north. Pinudjem claimed kingship and this shabti features his name in a cartouche.

Soldiers armed with bows and arrows and axes

Tomb of local governor Amenemhat, Beni Hassan, Egypt. 1965–1920 BC. Painted limestone

The unity of Egypt was the foundation of Egyptian kingship, but the country fragmented under the final weak Old Kingdom rulers. During the First Intermediate Period civil war and subsequent reunification scenes of soldiers and battles were common in tombs.

Stela of Tjetji (below and detail opposite)

Thebes, Egypt. 2125–2055 BC. Limestone, H 148 cm, W 110.5 cm

During the First Intermediate Period civil war, Tjetji held an important government position under the rulers who governed Upper Egypt. The long text describes his loyal service and the borders of the area controlled by these rulers.

Head of Pharaoh Mentuhotep II

Temple of Mentuhotep II, Deir el-Bahri, Thebes, Egypt. 2055–2004 BC. Sandstone, H 77 cm, W 21 cm

Pharaoh Mentuhotep II reunited the Two Lands of Upper and Lower Egypt after a long period of civil war. Here he wears the white crown of Upper Egypt, while associated statues wore the red crown of Lower Egypt.

'Make many monuments for God; this makes the name of him who does it live. Make the offering tables flourish, make the provisions great, increase the daily offerings! It is a good thing for him who does it'

The Teaching for King Merikare

He who builds the mansions of the gods

'Look, a vile deed happened in my time: the sacred province of Thinis was destroyed. It happened, but not as my action, and I knew of it only after it was done. See my shortcoming, which is pre-eminent in what I did'

The Teaching for King Merikare

He who builds the mansions of the gods

In Egypt temples were intended to serve as homes for the gods; the ancient Egyptian word for temple, *per netjer*, literally means 'house of god'. A statue of the god resided there and was cared for daily: washed, dressed, anointed with perfume and cosmetics and given food and drink. All temples depicted these activities being carried out by the king, but in reality this would not have been feasible. Most religious duties at temples throughout the country would have been carried out by priests acting on the king's behalf.

The kings were also responsible for building the temples themselves. Some pharaohs took a shortcut to fulfilling this duty by appropriating other kings' monuments, either adding to existing buildings or actually dismantling them, re-carving the blocks and reusing them. The poem 'The Teaching for King Merikare' encourages royal restoration but denounces destructive reuse (although it was not uncommon), stating that

a king 'should act for his predecessor for love of his achievements being restored by another succeeding him', while also exhorting 'Destroy not the monuments of another; you should hew new stone in Tura quarry!'

Ostensibly temples were built to serve and honour the gods but in reality they were as much for the benefit of the pharaoh. Temple decoration always depicts the gods in the company of the king, portrayed as a relationship of equals. A few rulers even dedicated temples to themselves and encouraged their own worship during their lifetimes; Amenhotep III, Seti I and Ramses II are all depicted offering to themselves in deified form.

Temples were dedicated to state gods associated with the pharaoh, but the general population focussed much of their worship on household deities, responsible for protecting the home or women in childbirth. Most people were probably not allowed into the temples anyway:

Temple pylon of Ptolemy XII (left)
Temple of Horus, Edfu, Egypt. 80–51 BC

Mud brick building ramp (above)
Temple of Amun, Karnak, Thebes, Egypt. 380–343 BC

access was reserved for the king along with priests and officials. Even when the statue of the god was paraded outside of the temple during festival processions it was still concealed within a shrine; no one but the king himself and his high priests had the privilege of looking upon the god.

In addition to the daily offerings to the gods, the pharaoh also gave gifts to the temples themselves: large tracts of land, foreign tributes and tax breaks. The Great Harris Papyrus (pp. 52–3) lists the extensive resources that Ramses III contributed to the temple of Amun-Ra at Thebes, including '421,362 cattle', '309,950 sacks of grain', '83 ships', '56 towns of Egypt and 9 foreign towns of Syria and Nubia'. Kings were praised for their generosity towards the gods, but their munificence was ultimately funded by their subjects' labour, and an increasing amount of it went towards the well-being of the powerful elite.

The wealth and influence of the priesthood of Amun in Thebes grew to such an extent that around 1069–945 BC the Theban High Priests of Amun actually took control of the southern half of Egypt, and the high priests Pinudjem and Menkherperra went so far as to claim kingship and write their names in cartouches.

Foreign rulers often sought support from the local priesthood and exploited the existing Egyptian religious system to gain acceptance for their rule. When faced with Egyptian rebellions the Macedonian-Greek child king Ptolemy V and his supporters made a deal with the priesthood for their support. They offered the temples tax breaks in exchange for their decreeing the deification of the boy king, which was recorded on the monument now known as the Rosetta Stone. Ultimately the king's responsibility to the gods was often reduced to the more worldly business of politics and finance.

Great Harris Papyrus

Thebes, Egypt. 1184–1153 BC. Papyrus, H 45.8 cm, L 76.5 cm

This papyrus describes Pharaoh Ramses III's achievements, including the construction of many temples and the extensive gifts he gave them. Here he stands before the gods of the main solar temple at Heliopolis.

Foundation deposit

Tomb of King Senkamanisken, Nuri, Sudan. 643–623 BC.
Red jasper, lapis lazuli, bronze, gold, calcite, faience and
chalcedony, H 1.7–5.5 cm, W 0.65–2.5 cm

During the construction of sacred buildings, foundation
deposits were placed under key parts of the structure.
Burying ritual objects like these tablets with the king's
cartouche or model building tools symbolically protected
the temple or tomb.

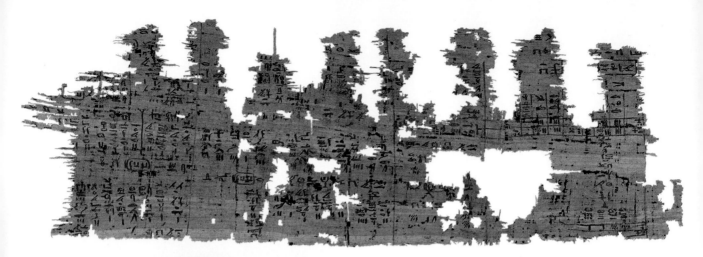

Abusir papyrus

Abusir, Egypt. 2494–2345 BC. Papyrus, H 28 cm, W 70 cm

The administrative archive of the royal memorial temples at Abusir gives us a glimpse of ancient Egypt's extensive bureaucracy and the ample resources controlled by temples. This papyrus records deliveries of grain and textiles and documents their storage.

Statue of the goddess Sekhmet

Karnak, Thebes, Egypt. 1390–1352 BC.
Granite, H 79 cm, W 50 cm

The lion goddess Sekhmet was the fierce daughter of the sun god Ra. Hundreds of such statues were dedicated to her in the memorial temple of Pharaoh Amenhotep III, suggesting the king sought her favour and protection.

Re-carved temple inscription

Bubastis, Egypt. Originally dated to 1874–1855 BC.
Red granite, H 98 cm, W 101 cm

This huge block originally bore the name of Pharaoh
Senusret III, but 600 years later the cartouche of Ramses II
was carved on top. Re-carving existing monuments was a
cost-effective method for kings building temples.

**Plaque of Amenemhat IV offering ointment
to Atum**
Byblos, Lebanon. 1808–1799 BC. Gold, H 3.1 cm, W 3.1 cm

The gods who resided in the temples had to be cared for and offered to daily, in theory by the king, in practice by priests. The daily ritual involved washing and dressing the divine statue, anointing it with perfume and cosmetics, offering food, such as bread, meat, fruit and vegetables, and drink, such as wine and milk, and burning incense for purification.

Offering stand with dishes and preserved food
Egypt. 1550–1186 BC. Papyrus, palm, bread, dom palm fruit, duck and linen

Stela of Tiberius, pharaoh and Roman emperor

Karnak, Thebes, Egypt. AD 14–37. Sandstone, H 66.5 cm, W 44.5 cm, D 9.5 cm

Foreign conquerors sought legitimacy in Egypt by adopting Egyptian customs and religion. This stela describes the renovation of the Karnak temple by Emperor Tiberius. He is depicted as a pharaoh, offering to the gods Mut and Khonsu, but in Rome Tiberius banned the worship of Egyptian gods.

When the Egyptians conquered Nubia (Sudan) they identified a mountain there, Jebel Barkal, as the birthplace and southern residence of their chief god Amun, justifying Egypt's control of the region. Later, Egypt fell into decline and civil war while local Nubian rulers rose in power. They identified Amun as their divine father and the pharaohs as their ancestors. They revived old traditions and took over Egypt, a move they viewed as a divinely-ordained liberation. Taharqa, the greatest Nubian pharaoh, was buried in a large pyramid near Jebel Barkal.

The sacred mountain of Jebel Barkal
Karima, Sudan

Shabti of Nubian Pharaoh Taharqa
Nuri, Sudan. 690–664 BC. Calcite, H 33.5 cm

Pharaohs were usually considered to be of divine descent, but only became gods when they died. Kings built and endowed temples for their own worship after their deaths but a few encouraged their veneration during their own lifetimes. Akhenaten went a step futher: he dismantled the existing Egyptian religion and instituted exclusive worship of the solar disc, the Aten, with himself serving as its intermediary. People could only practise the religion through worshipping Akhenaten and his family. The stela below, which features his parents, takes the form of a shrine for this purpose.

Trial-piece with head of Pharaoh Akhenaten (detail, right)
Amarna, Egypt. 1352–1336 BC.
Limestone, H 16.7 cm, W 13.5 cm

Stela of Pharaoh Amenhotep III and Queen Tiy (below)
Amarna, Egypt. 1352– 1336 BC.
Limestone, H 32.5 cm, W 29.3 cm

*'He is a hero, active with his strong arm,
a champion without compare. None can escape his
arrow, none draw his bow. As before the power of
the Great One, barbarians flee before him'*

The Tale of Sinuhe

A champion without compare

---

*'When Menna, my shield bearer, saw that a large
number of chariots surrounded us, he became weak
and faint-hearted…We stood alone in the midst of
battle, abandoned by soldiers and chariotry'*

The poem of the Battle of Kadesh

A champion without compare

The pharaohs presented an impressive image of themselves as warrior-kings, defending Egypt by conquering her potential enemies. Certain kings were undoubtedly good military leaders, some having served as generals before succeeding to the throne. But ultimately they all relied on the soldiers in their army to win their battles, some of whom were actually mercenaries from the very countries that Egypt traditionally viewed as enemies.

Like many cultures, the Egyptians were not inclined to document failure. The poem of the Battle of Kadesh, written from the point of view of Ramses II, tells of his extraordinary, single-handed triumph against the army of the Anatolian Hittite Empire. However, Hittite records tell a different story, suggesting that the outcome was actually a truce. Kadesh remained in Hittite hands and a peace treaty was signed, but despite this, Ramses II managed to masterfully retell the event as a glorious victory, making him renowned as a great military leader and securing his future name of Ramses the Great.

Pharaohs characterized their military campaigns and empire building as a way of upholding *ma'at* and defending Egypt's borders, but what really drove their desire for conquest was the acquisition of valuable resources. Gold from Nubia was especially prized. A letter from King Tushratta of Mitanni, who was allied with Egypt, demands more gold to buy his country's loyalty, claiming, 'in my brother's country, gold is as plentiful as dust'.

Pharaohs stressed their role as warriors, but diplomacy was just as important to Egypt's foreign policy. Diplomatic alliances were forged through correspondence, elaborate gift-giving and diplomatic marriages. Egyptian pharaohs married the daughters of foreign rulers to cement their treaties, but Amenhotep III responded to the

Kushite Royal Pyramids
Meroe, Sudan. 300 BC–AD 350

Pyramids continued to be built by Nubian kings hundreds of years after Egypt's occupation of Nubia and subsequent defeat at the hands of the Nubian kings.

Babylonian king's request for an Egyptian bride by saying, 'from old, the daughter of an Egyptian king has not been given in marriage to anyone'.

Egypt labelled its traditional enemies 'the Nine Bows' – chiefly the Nubians to the south, the Asiatics to the east and the Libyans to the west, as well as the Hyksos, Hittites, Mitanni, Assyrians and Persians. Enemy nations were generally represented by stereotypical depictions of individual captives, each personifying an entire people. Nations had derogatory epithets attached to them; Egyptian texts refer to 'wretched Kush' and 'vile Asiatics'. This outward hostility and negative stereotyping strengthened Egyptian unity and sense of identity, but in reality many foreigners freely lived and worked in Egypt, even in important positions.

Although the pharaohs proudly proclaimed their military victories, their failures were just as numerous, if less well documented. Egypt was frequently invaded by external powers, resulting in the rule of foreign pharaohs for almost a third of Egyptian history: including the Hyksos, Libyans, Nubians, Assyrians, Persians, Macedonian-Greeks and Romans. The kings of Kush, from Nubia, took inspiration from Egyptian royal tombs and built more royal pyramids in Sudan than are found in Egypt itself. After hundreds of years of occupation by the pharaohs, the Nubians' familiarity with Egyptian traditions was an asset which they used to their advantage when they invaded and took control of Egypt for themselves.

War was always a dangerous business, never as simple and clean as the effortless victories depicted on temple walls. King Seqenenra Taa II ruled over southern Egypt until he challenged the foreign Hyksos ruler for control of the north; evidently killed in battle, Seqenenra's skull bears ugly wounds from the multiple axe blows and arrow wounds that spelled his end.

Cast of a scene of Ramses II conquering Nubia in a war chariot
Cast of Beit el-Wali Temple, Egypt. 1278–1213 BC

Axe

El-Mostagedda, Egypt. 1650–1550 BC. Bronze, wood, and leather, L 41.1 cm, W (cutting edge) 6.3 cm

Axes were common weapons of the Egyptian infantry, who bore the brunt of the fighting in pharaohs' military campaigns. This one may have been used for ceremonial purposes as it is inscribed with the throne name of a pharaoh, 'Neb-maat-ra'.

Sphinx (fore part) holding a captive

Abydos, Egypt. 1985–1795 BC. Ivory, L 5.6 cm

The sphinx was a symbol of the power and strength of the pharaoh. This statuette depicts the king as a sphinx seizing a captive, probably a Nubian, one of Egypt's traditional enemies.

Block statue of Inebny

Thebes, Egypt. 1479–1425 BC.
Limestone, L 153 cm, W 112 cm

Inebny served as a troop commander and
overseer of weaponry. The inscription states
that he 'followed his lord' on expeditions to
foreign lands, probably the highly successful
campaigns of King Thutmose III in Nubia
and Syria.

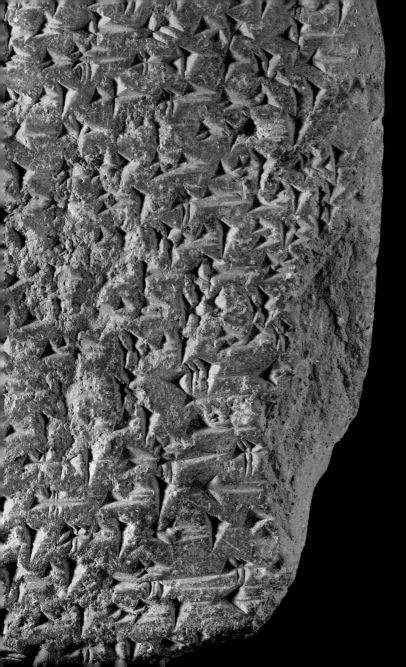

The pharaoh emphasized his military might, but surviving royal correspondence demonstrates that diplomatic solutions were regularly sought in the increasingly interconnected Mediterranean world. Diplomatic exchanges range from the grovelling submission of small city-state Irqata to demands for valuable gifts from the King of Babylon. Akkadian, rather than Egyptian, was the international language of diplomacy in this period.

Cuneiform tablet letter from a Babylonian king
Amarna, Egypt. 1352–1336 BC. Clay, L 13.5 cm, W 7 cm

Scarab depicting Pharaoh Thutmose I in battle
Egypt. 1504–1492 BC. Green jasper, L 1.53 cm, W 1.12 cm

This scarab depicts Thutmose I shooting a Nubian soldier from a chariot, a form of military technology that had only been recently introduced to Egypt by their enemies from the Near East.

Cuneiform tablet letter from the city-state of Irqata

Amarna, Egypt. 1352–1336 BC . Clay, L 9 cm, W 6.5 cm

Relief fragment of a battle scene

Temple of Mentuhotep II, Deir el-Bahri, Thebes, Egypt.
2055–2004 BC. Limestone, H 60 cm, W 66 cm

Shrine door of Persian ruler Darius I

Egypt. 522–486 BC. Wood, glass, H 28 cm, W 3.5 cm

Images of defeated enemies were a common decorative element on Egyptian temples. Above, under siege in a Near Eastern walled city, Asiatic defenders fall to their death, pierced by arrows. However, Egypt was not as consistently victorious as their depictions of battles would suggest, and conquering foreign rulers often presided over the very temples that depicted their defeat. The 'Asiatic' Persian King Darius I depicted himself as a traditional pharaoh – here he is shown offering to the gods Anubis and Isis – but while his army was fighting in Greece he faced a revolt in Egypt.

Tile depicting a captive Libyan chief (left)
Tell el-Yahudiya, Egypt. 1184–1153 BC. Faience, H 31 cm, W 9.1 cm

Tile depicting a Nubian captive (above)
Tell el-Yahudiya, Egypt. 1184–1153 BC. Faience, H 15.9 cm, W 8.7 cm

These tiles come from a palace of Ramses III and might have been placed near the base of the pharaoh's throne so he could symbolically trample his enemies. Foreigners were always depicted as stereotypes of an entire ethnic group rather than individuals. Each nation was given distinctive characteristics and exaggerated features to distinguish them from the Egyptians. However, in their own art these peoples depicted themselves very differently.

Head of a Nubian pharaoh

Probably Heliopolis, Egypt. 716–702 BC. Granite, H 16.5 cm, W 15 cm

The Kushite kings of Nubia, who conquered Egypt and ruled as pharaohs,
combined Nubian features and Egyptian iconography in their representations.
Originally this statue would have been gilded and it probably represents
Nubian Pharaoh Shabako wearing an Egyptian *nemes* headdress.

Lord of Eternity

Lord of Eternity

The cycle of kingship came full circle with the death of the king and the coronation of his successor. As a new king became the next incarnation of Horus, the deceased king was thought to transform into Osiris, ruler of the afterlife, as well as joining with the sun god Ra on his nightly journey through the underworld. But even from beyond the grave the influence and reputation of a king could live on long after their death in the memories of the Egyptian people.

The king's memorialization began with his burial. Whether interred in a pyramid or a rock-cut tomb in the Valley of the Kings, pharaohs could be accompanied to the grave by a rich assortment of luxury goods to provide for them in the afterlife, from food and gilded furniture to chariots and board games.

The tomb, and the funerary texts and images that decorated it, acted as a vehicle to transform the deceased king into the divine – to unite with the sun and to become Osiris. The tomb of Djer (c. 3100 BC), one of the earliest kings, was later identified by the Egyptians as the tomb of the god Osiris, the mythological first king of Egypt, and became a place of pilgrimage. But despite grand aspirations for the afterlife, most rulers suffered an ignoble end. Tomb robbery was rife; dozens of rulers from the latter half of the second millennium BC ended up stacked in a pile of bodies in a tomb at Deir el-Bahri after priests gathered the mummies for safekeeping. Papyri record several trials of the tomb robbers and their accounts of theft and destruction.

Nevertheless, the royal funerary temples ensured their worship after death. Depending on the popularity of the pharaoh and the wealth of his funerary endowments, certain cults lasted for hundreds of years. The manner in which kings were remembered owed something to the success of their reign and how well they engineered their public persona, which could be reinforced by

Statue of Pharaoh Mentuhotep II
Egypt. 1550–1295 BC. Limestone, H 24.2 cm, W 11 cm

Dedicated over 500 years after his death, this mummiform statue of King Mentuhotep II depicts him as Osiris, ruler of the afterlife.

official eulogising texts, or subverted in popular literature. Ramses II reigned for sixty-six years, leaving behind numerous monuments and a legacy in the shadow of which his successors lived for the next four centuries; eleven subsequent kings of that period modelled their names on his.

The image of the pharaoh depicted through statues and temples was all-powerful, but was less secure in the written word. King Khufu is memorialized by the unparalleled grandeur of his funerary monument, the Great Pyramid; however this same monument perhaps suggested to Egyptians living long after his reign that his great building achievement might have been accomplished through tyranny. In one series of humorous stories, Khufu appears as cruelly insensitive in his readiness to put a prisoner to death for the sake of a magic trick.

Literature could be used to question the role of the king but the pharaohs also recognized the enduring power of words, as the 'Teaching for King Merikare' so eloquently demonstrates. In this poem, the pharaoh instructs his son in a lesson for the ages:

'Be skilful with words, and you will be victorious.
The strong arm of the king is his tongue.
Words are stronger than any weapon…
Emulate your forefathers, your ancestors…
Look, their words endure in writings.
Open, and read, and emulate the wise!'

So the voices of the pharaohs have survived through the ages and continue to captivate with their fascinating, but often contradictory, legacy.

The Tomb of Tutankhamun
Valley of the Kings, Thebes, Egypt. 1327 BC.
Photograph by Harry Burton, 1922

One of several rooms in the tomb, filled
with items including furniture and chariots
for the pharaoh's use in the afterlife.

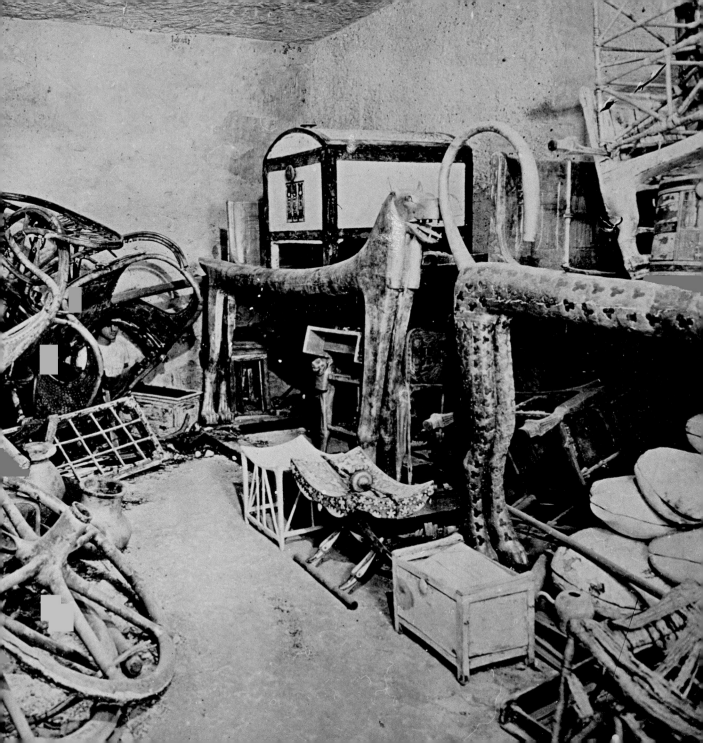

Tomb robbery account in the Abbott Papyrus

Thebes, Egypt. 1099–1069 BC. Papyrus, L 218 cm, W 42.5 cm (now divided into three frames)

This document records an investigation into allegations of tomb robbery during the reign of Ramses IX and the trial of thieves found guilty of robbing the tomb of King Sobekemzaf II. Some robberies were even part of a government policy to recover gold and precious materials from the Valley of the Kings and nearby.

Shabti of Pharaoh Seti I

Tomb of Seti I, Valley of the Kings, Thebes, Egypt. 1294–1279 BC. Faience, H 22.8 cm, W 9.6 cm

The pharaoh's preparations for death were similar to others' in some respects. Egyptians believed in an afterlife that was a continuation of their everyday life, in which individuals could be called upon to perform agricultural labour. Shabtis were placed in the tomb to perform the work required of the deceased – pharaohs had hundreds of these figurines.

Guardian figure of Pharaoh Ramses I

Tomb of Ramses I, Valley of the Kings, Thebes, Egypt.
1295–1294 BC. Sycamore wood and bitumen,
H 218 cm, W 57 cm

Tomb guardian statues were placed on either side of doors
within the royal tomb to protect the chambers beyond.
The black colour (now mostly lost) of this huge statue of
Pharaoh Ramses I is symbolic of Osiris and rebirth, like
the dark fertile soil of the Nile Valley. Originally it would
have been embellished with gold foil and the eyes and
eyebrows inlaid with precious materials.

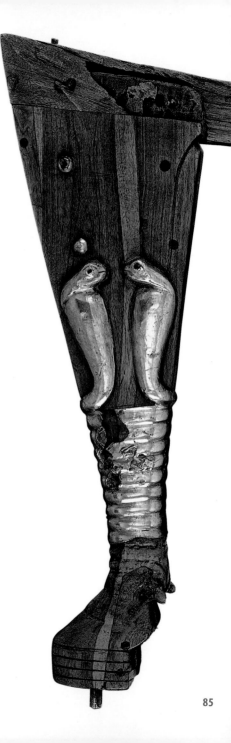

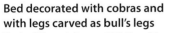

Bed decorated with cobras and with legs carved as bull's legs

Tomb of Pharaoh Ramses IX, Valley of the Kings, Thebes, Egypt. 1126–1069 BC. Wood, gold and silver, W 2.9 cm, L (each leg) 7.5 cm

New Kingdom pharaohs were buried with the finest goods to meet all their needs in the afterlife. This bed is from the tomb of King Ramses IX, but may have originally been made much earlier. The bull and cobra were symbols of royal power.

Stela of Neferhotep (left)

Karnak, Thebes, Egypt. 1295–1186 BC. Limestone, H 46.5 cm, W 30.5 cm

Neferhotep was foreman of the workmen who constructed and decorated the royal tombs in the Valley of the Kings. This stela shows his adoration for Pharaoh Amenhotep I and Queen Ahmose-Nefertari who, several centuries earlier, founded the workmen's village of Deir el-Medina, where they were deified and thought to be able to intervene in everyday life.

Stela depicting royal statues (above)

Temple of Mentuhotep II, Deir el-Bahri, Thebes, Egypt. 1504–1295 BC. Limestone, H 35 cm, W 42.5 cm

Mentuhotep II was renowned for reunifying Egypt after its first civil war and numerous pharaohs sought to associate themselves with him. Amenhotep I was one of the first kings to govern a recently reunited Egypt after a period of foreign invasion and divided rule. He presented himself as a reunifier by erecting similar statues in the temple of Mentuhotep II. The statue of Amenhotep I pictured here is also depicted on a stela (left) alongside statues of Mentuhotep II, all shown in the form of Osiris, ruler of the Underworld.

Statue of Amenhotep I in Osiris form
Temple of Mentuhotep II, Deir el-Bahri, Thebes, Egypt. 1525–1504 BC. Limestone, H 269 cm

Ostracon featuring part of the 'Tale of Sinuhe'

Thebes, Egypt. 1295–1186 BC. Ink on limestone,
H 17 cm, W 30 cm

In this story Sinuhe, an official, flees Egypt after the
assassination of Pharaoh Amenemhat I and lives in
exile until he is summoned home again in his old
age. The tale explores the relationship between the
individual and the pharaoh, who is presented as
fearsome and forgiving.

Statue of Pharaoh Senusret III (left)

Elephantine, Egypt. 1874–1855 BC.
Graywacke, H 22 cm, W 14 cm

Senusret III, one of Egypt's greatest empire builders,
was renowned as a hero king, yet he chose to balance
this image with poems extoling both his military
prowess and his caring love for his subjects, along
with sculpture, such as this statue, depicting him as
careworn through concern for his people.

Statue of Pharaoh Ramses II (right)

Temple of Khnum, Elephantine, Egypt. 1279–1213 BC.
Granite, H 143 cm, W 68 cm

The monumental statuary of Ramses the Great
presents him as an imposing, all-powerful ruler, but
also inspired Shelley's poem 'Ozymandias': "'My name
is Ozymandias, King of kings: / Look on my works, ye
mighty, and despair!' / Nothing beside remains. Round
the decay / Of that colossal wreck, boundless and bare,
/ The lone and level sands stretch far away'.

Sunset over the Nile

At death, the pharaoh united with the setting
sun and was born again at dawn as a new ruler:
so Egyptian kingship continued with the same
constancy as the annual Nile flood, despite
many challenges to its survival. But finally, under
Byzantine rule, the royal traditions and even the
knowledge of hieroglyphs died out, and the sun
set on over 3000 years of civilization.

Glossary

Amun, also Amun-Ra: one of the chief Egyptian national gods; originally just a local deity worshipped in Thebes, he rose to pre-eminence when the Theban pharaohs came to power and was often linked with the sun god Ra.

ankh: the hieroglyphic sign for 'life', often used as a protective symbol, which takes the form of a T-shape surmounted by a loop.

block statue: a statue of a non-royal person, usually covered by a cloak, seated on the ground with their crossed arms resting on their drawn-up knees. This statue type economized on stone and provided a large surface for a hieroglyphic inscription.

cartouche: an oval with a horizontal line at one end used to indicate that the enclosed text is a royal name. Its shape derives from the shen ring, a symbol of eternal protection.

cuneiform: a script developed in Mesopotamia, written with wedge-shaped impressions on clay tablets and used for languages such as Sumerian and Akkadian.

faience: a glazed ceramic material made of crushed quartz or quartz sand with small amounts of lime and plant ash or natron, most often produced in a blue-green colour.

Horus: a falcon god, son of Osiris and Isis, associated with the sky, divine kingship and the reigning pharaoh.

Isis: a protective goddess, wife of Osiris and mother of Horus, who protected the king, the deceased, and those in need of magical-medical aid.

Lower Egypt: a term used to designate the northern part of Egypt, the Delta region from ancient Memphis northwards, where the Nile fans out into a number of tributaries across an alluvial plain.

ma'at: an Egyptian concept suggesting the established order of the world and balance of the universe.

Ma'at: the goddess who personified the concept of ma'at, depicted as a woman wearing an ostrich feather on her head.

nemes headdress: a headcloth of linen with two lappets at the shoulders, gathered in a tail at the back of the head, worn by the pharaoh.

Osiris: originally a fertility god, he was important in Egyptian religion as the mythical first king of Egypt and ruler of the afterlife.

ostracon: a limestone or pottery fragment used as a writing or drawing surface.

palette: a stone slab used for grinding cosmetic pigments, or sometimes carved with ceremonial reliefs for royal ritual purposes during the Early Dynastic period.

Ra: the sun god and chief Egyptian deity, whose universal nature meant he was often manifest in other important gods (e.g. Ra-Horakhty, Amun-Ra) and depicted in a variety of ways, such as a ram or a hawk-headed human.

red crown: the distinctive tall stepped crown of Lower Egypt with a projecting curled wire.

scarab: a sacred dung beetle associated with the sun god, a form often used for amulets or seals.

sed-festival: a royal jubilee celebrating a renewal of the king's powers, often performed after the first thirty years of a king's rule.

Seth: brother of the god Osiris, whom he murdered for the throne only to be defeated by his nephew Horus, the rightful heir; an ambivalent god associated with chaos and deserts, but whose negative powers could also be harnessed for good.

shabti: a funerary figurine, inscribed with a magical spell, which was placed in the tomb to stand in for the deceased if they were called upon to perform physical labour in the afterlife.

shendyt-kilt: a knee-length kilt made of fine pleated linen wrapped around the waist with a distinctive central panel. Its wear was initially restricted to the king, but it eventually came to be worn by non-royal individuals as well.

Two Lands: the ancient Egyptians conceived of their country as made up of the two geographically distinct regions of Upper and Lower Egypt, which they believed were first united under the rule of King Narmer. It was the king's duty as 'Lord of the Two Lands' to maintain the unity of the nation.

Upper Egypt: a term used to designate the southern part of Egypt, from ancient Memphis southwards, consisting of a narrow ribbon of fertile land bounded by desert cliffs.

uraeus: a rearing cobra, symbolic of royal power, most typically worn on the brow of the pharaoh. The cobra was associated with Wadjet, the goddess of Lower Egypt.

white crown: the distinctive tall conical crown associated with Upper Egypt.

vizier: a pharaoh's most important government official.

Further reading

Baines, John, and Jaromir Malek, *Cultural Atlas of Ancient Egypt*. New York: Checkmark Books, 2000.

Freed, Rita E., Yvonne J. Markowitz, and Sue H. D'Auria (eds), *Pharaohs of the Sun: Akhenaten – Nefertiti – Tutankhamen*. New York: Bulfinch Press, 1999.

Kemp, Barry, *Egypt: Anatomy of a Civilisation*. London: Routledge, 2nd edition 2006.

Lehner, Mark, *The Complete Pyramids*. London: Thames and Hudson, 1997.

Lichtheim, Miriam, *Ancient Egyptian Literature*, vols. 1–3. Berkley: University of California Press, 2nd edition 2006.

O'Connor, David, and David P. Silverman (eds), *Ancient Egyptian Kingship*. Leiden: E. J. Brill, 1995.

Parkinson, Richard B., *The Tale of Sinuhe and Other Ancient Egyptian Poems 1940–1640 BC*, Oxford: Oxford University Press, reprinted 2009.

Parkinson, Richard B., *Voices of Ancient Egypt: An Anthology of Middle Kingdom Writings*, London: British Museum Press, reprinted 2008.

Quirke, Stephen, *Who Were the Pharaohs?* London: British Museum Press, revised edition 2010.

Shaw, Ian (ed.), *The Oxford History of Ancient Egypt*. Oxford: Oxford University Press, 2000.

Acknowledgements

This book was inspired by the touring exhibition *Pharaoh: King of Egypt*, developed in a partnership between Tyne & Wear Archives & Museums and the British Museum, supported through the generosity of the Dorset Foundation. I would like to take this opportunity to thank everyone involved in the project at the British Museum, especially Dr Neal Spencer, Keeper of Ancient Egypt and Sudan, as well as all of the exhibition partners, particularly Tyne & Wear Archives & Museums, notably Sarah Glynn, Gill Scott, Steve McLean and the staff of the Great North Museum: Hancock. My sincere thanks to the Department of Ancient Egypt and Sudan at the British Museum for their invaluable support, encouragement and expertise: Vivian Davies, Marcel Marée, John Taylor, Susanne Woodhouse, Derek Welsby, Julie Anderson, Daniel Antoine, Elisabeth O'Connell, Patricia Usick, Claire Messenger, Emily Taylor, Simon Prentice, Mark Haswell, Evan York, Tania Watkins, Tom Haynes, Alex Garrett, Claire Thorne, Shezza Edris and Alicja Sliwinska.

This book was written while I was participating in the British Museum Future Curators programme and also completing a D.Phil. at Oxford University. I am very grateful for the patience and encouragement of my doctoral supervisors and mentors Professor John Baines at Oxford University and Dr Richard Parkinson at the British Museum, whom I must also thank for most of the elegant translations of ancient Egyptian literature that appear in this book. My thanks also to everyone involved with the Future Curators programme at both the British Museum and Great North Museum: Hancock, especially Maria Bojanowska, Andrew Parkin and the Heritage Lottery Fund, as well as my fellow participants, Morn Capper, Qin Cao, Amelia Tubelli and Oliver Spiers. Thanks to all my amazing colleagues and friends from Oxford and elsewhere, especially Dr Maria Cannata and Marie Vandenbeusch.

Special thanks to my partner Adrian Hon, for his patience and inspiration, and to my wonderful family who have always supported my passion for ancient Egypt: my parents John and Robin Maitland, my sisters Catherine and Heather Maitland, and my grandparents James and Elma LaForce.

Image credits

Except where otherwise stated, photographs are © The Trustees of the British Museum. British Museum inventory numbers are listed below. Further information about the Museum and its collection can be found at britishmuseum.org.

pp.1 and 36 EA 16518
pp.2–3 and 22 EA 1450 Donated by Egypt Exploration Fund
p.4 EA 2280
p.6 Map drawn by David Hoxley
p.8 Photograph by Kenneth Garrett/ National Geographic/Getty Images
p.9 EA 986
p.10 EA 9953,B1
p.11 EA 117
pp.14–15 © Margaret Maitland
pp.16–17 and 19 EA 54460
p.20 EA 60756
p.21 EA 1006 Donated by Egypt Exploration Fund
p.23 EA 5602 Donated by Sir John Gardner Wilkinson
p.23 EA 552
p.24 EA 60006
p.25 GR 1861,1127.135
p.26 EA 54388
p.26 EA 1015 Donated by Sir Charles Holland Smith
p.27 EA 174
pp.28–9 EA 10182,2
p.29 EA 57348
p.30 EA 65429
p.30 EA 1209
p.31 EA 58953 Donated by C.W. Scott

pp.32 and 46 EA 720 Donated by Egypt Exploration Fund
p.35 EA 12835
p.37 EA 11109
pp.38 and 39 EA 35714
p.40 Photograph by Graham Harrison
p.41 EA 32650 Donated by Egypt Exploration Fund
p.42 EA 48
p.42 EA 5620
p.43 EA 34178
pp.44–5 © Margaret Maitland
pp.46 and 47 EA 614
p.48 EA 64564 Donated by Marion Whiteford Acworth JP
p.51 Photograph by Graham Harrison
p.51 © Neal Spencer
pp.52–3 EA 9999,24
p.53 EA 55561 Donated by the Government of Sudan
p.54 EA 10735,9
p.54 EA 79
p.55 EA 1102 Donated by Egypt Exploration Fund
p.56 EA 59194 Donated by Birmingham Jewellers' and Silversmiths' Association
p.57 EA 36191
EA 5368
EA 45292
EA 5340
EA 5341
p.58 EA 398
p.58 EA 55483 Donated by the Government of Sudan
p.59 © Adrian Hon
p.60 EA 57399 Donated by Egypt

Exploration Fund
p.61 EA 63631 Donated by Egypt Exploration Fund
pp.62 and 66–7 Cast of a scene from Beit el-Wali Temple, Egypt. British Museum.
p.65 © Margaret Maitland
p.68 EA 63224
p.68 EA 54678 Donated by Mrs Russell Rea
p.69 EA 1131
p.70 E29825
p.70 EA 17774
p.71 E29786
p.72 EA 732 Donated by Egypt Exploration Fund
p.73 EA 37496
p.74 EA 12337
p.74 EA 12293
p.75 EA 638331 Donated by Barlow Webb
pp.76 and 84 EA 854
p.79 EA 53890
pp.80–1 Private Collection/The Stapleton Collection/The Bridgeman Art Library
p.82 EA 10221
p.83 EA 22818 Donated by Arthur Lyttelton Annesley
p.85 EA 21574 Donated by Jesse Haworth
p.86 EA 1516
p.86 EA 690 Donated by Egypt Exploration Fund
p.87 EA 683 Donated by Egypt Exploration Fund
p.88 EA 36298
p.88 EA 5629
p.89 EA 67 Donated by William Richard Hamilton
pp.90–1 © Margaret Maitland

Index